Mit Wörterbuch und Vokabelhilfe

Klaus-Peter Wolf

Englisch lernen mit den Leselöwen Pferdegeschichten

Aus dem Deutschen übersetzt von David Ingram
Zeichnungen von Irmtraut Teltau

Bibliografische Information Der Deutschen Bibliothek
Die Deutsche Bibliothek verzeichnet diese Publikation in der
Deutschen Nationalbibliografie; detaillierte bibliografische Daten
sind im Internet über *http://dnb.ddb.de* abrufbar.

Der Umwelt zuliebe ist dieses Buch
auf chlorfrei gebleichtem Papier gedruckt.

ISBN 3-7855-4787-0 – 1. Auflage 2003
© 2003 Loewe Verlag GmbH, Bindlach
Die deutsche Originalausgabe erschien 1993 im Loewe
Verlag unter dem Titel „Leselöwen-Pferdegeschichten"
Aus dem Deutschen übersetzt von David Ingram
Umschlagillustration: Irmtraut Teltau
Umschlaggestaltung: Andreas Henze
Gesamtherstellung: sachsendruck, Plauen
Printed in Germany

www.loewe-verlag.de

Contents

Pauline goes as red as a tomato 11
Max and Maxi 18
Peter's pipe-cleaner horse 26
Tinka and the lollipop 34
Prinz and the horse with horns 42
Jan looks after the horses 48
The tracker 56

Liebe Eltern,

unaufhaltsam hält die englische Sprache Einzug in den kindlichen Wortschatz. Was die Sprachwissenschaft nüchtern als Anglizismen betitelt, finden die Kinder überaus spannend. Mit ungebremstem Wissensdurst machen sie sich daran, erste Worte oder Sätze in einer Fremdsprache zu erlernen und zu kommunizieren.

Kinder sind relativ früh mit dem Englischen vertraut, spätestens seit der Einführung des Englischunterrichts an den Grundschulen. Eine Fremdsprache spielerisch, ohne Erfolgszwang, dafür aber mit schnellen Erfolgserlebnissen lernen, so lautet das Motto.
Dieses Prinzip haben wir auch den Englisch-Ausgaben unserer Erstlese-Reihe *Leselöwen* zu Grunde gelegt. In abgeschlossenen Geschichten können die kindlichen Leser ihre ersten Englischkenntnisse anwenden und vertiefen. Die Sprache ist einfach gehalten, die wichtigsten Vokabeln sind im Text markiert und werden in ihrer konkreten Bedeutung am Rand auf Deutsch erklärt. Verben werden dabei gleich in der jeweiligen Person, Adjektive in der flektierten

Form übersetzt. Der Sinn eines Satzes lässt sich so schnell und ohne lästiges Nachschlagen erschließen. Viele Begriffe werden zusätzlich in den Illustrationen durch Wort-Bildzuweisungen erläutert.

Im Anhang finden sich sowohl die wichtigsten Vokabeln aus dem Text in alphabetischer Reihenfolge als auch ein speziell dem jeweiligen Thema zu Grunde gelegter Wortschatz auf einer praktischen Ausklappseite.

Die Verben stehen hier im Infinitiv, da an dieser Stelle der Hauptakzent eher auf der Erweiterung des Wortschatzes als auf der Erschließung eines Wortes innerhalb eines Satzes liegt. Dabei werden nicht alle möglichen Bedeutungen im Deutschen angegeben, sondern nur die wichtigsten.

Und wenn Sie mit Ihrem Kind gleichzeitig auch das Hörverständnis und die Sprechfertigkeit trainieren möchten, sind bei Jumbo zu jedem englischen *Leselöwen*-Band die entsprechenden Hörkassetten erhältlich.

Viel Spaß und Erfolg mit
„Englisch lernen mit den Leselöwen"
wünscht Ihnen Ihr

Leselöwen-Englisch-Team

Pauline goes as red as a tomato

Pauline is at the riding stable. *Reitstall*
She is sad. She wants to see the horses, to feed them and to stroke them. But instead, she *streicheln; stattdessen*
must clean the stable. And the *sauber machen*
stable really stinks! Poo! *wirklich*
 Pauline carries the dirty straw *trägt; Stroh*
outside with her pitchfork. *Heugabel*
She wants to hold her nose. *sich die Nase zuhalten*
But she needs both hands *braucht*
to carry the pitchfork. *tragen*
 "What a stinky job," Pauline thinks. She is angry. "It is nicer *wütend; schöner*
to clean my room. At least, my *Wenigstens*
room doesn't smell so horrible!" *schrecklich*
 Then Mr Jokel comes into the stable. He owns the horses, *Ihm gehören*
the stable and the meadow. *Weide*
He always wears riding boots *Reitstiefel*
and a black cap. *schwarze Kappe*

Mr Jokel looks around the stable. Then he smiles. "You clean the stable very well. Do you clean up your room at home like this, too?"

Mr Jokel does not realize that Pauline is upset.

Pauline sometimes gets so upset that she breathes in very quickly. Then she starts to stammer. And then she feels so ashamed that she goes as red as a tomato.

Her brother Jens often laughs at her about that: "Ha ha! Tomato-Pauline!"

Pauline is worried. She does not want to stammer. She says nothing. But she goes as red as a tomato.

Mr Jokel does not notice. He holds out his hand to her with a smile and says:

Stall; lächelt
machst sauber; sehr gut

so

bemerkt

verärgert

atmet ein

stottern

beschämt

Tomate

besorgt

bemerkt
streckt aus

"Do you want to ride a real horse?"

Pauline stares at the floor and shakes her head.

"How terrible," she thinks. "My face is as red as a tomato again."

She is frightened and ashamed and does not know why.

echtes	
starrt	
schüttelt den Kopf	
schrecklich	
fürchtet sich	
schämt sich	

"Come on," Mr Jokel says. "Basta wants to meet you. Basta is a stallion. He likes girls like you."

Now Pauline takes Mr Jokel's hand. But she does not look at him.

Mr Jokel and Pauline go to the meadow.

Hengst

Weide

"Look!" Mr Jokel says. "There is Basta! He likes to chase butterflies. But he doesn't eat them. He only sniffs at them. The butterflies don't know that, so they are frightened. They fly away. Call him! Then he comes."

jagen
Schmetterlinge
schnuppert

fürchten sich
fliegen weg

"I don't think so," Pauline thinks. "I'm as red as a tomato. That frightens horses."

macht Angst

"Call him!" Mr Jokel says again.

Pauline shuts her eyes and then calls: "Basta! Basta!"

schließt die Augen

"Louder! You must shout louder. He can't hear you."

Pauline wants to run away. But then she decides to shout very loudly: "Basta! Come here immediately!"

beschließt

sofort

Pauline cannot believe her eyes. Basta neighs and then gallops over to her! He waits in front of her. Pauline strokes Basta's head.

Pauline looks proudly at Mr Jokel. Her face is not red anymore.

Pauline realizes that Basta obeys her. He does not care about her red face.

"C… c… can you teach me to ride him?" Pauline asks.

Mr Jokel nods. "Of course! Let's start immediately."

Ten months later, Pauline is a brave rider. She never stammers when she talks to Basta. Pauline's brother goes as red as a tomato now because he is frightened of Basta. And he is jealous that his sister is such a good rider!

ihren Augen trauen
wiehert; galloppiert
herüber
streichelt

stolz

nicht mehr
bemerkt
gehorcht
kümmert sich um

nickt; Natürlich
sofort
später
mutige Reiterin
stottert

fürchtet sich
eifersüchtig

Max and Maxi

Max is a fairground horse. It costs one euro to ride on him.
   Max is good to children. He never throws them off his back. Sometimes the children move around a lot in the saddle. Some of them hang on to his mane and that hurts. But Max is always patient.

Kirmespferd	
kostet einen Euro	
wirft sie nie von seinem Rücken ab	
zappeln	
Sattel	
klammern; Mähne	
tut weh	
geduldig	

mane

One little girl likes Max a lot. Her name is Maxi.

She knows a place on Max's back where Max likes to be scratched. | Stelle; Rücken

gekratzt werden

Maxi scratches Max and Max is very happy. | kratzt

But Maxi cannot ride all day on Max because each ride costs one euro. | jeder Ritt

kostet einen Euro

One thing Max doesn't like are his blinkers. They force him to look straight ahead. | Scheuklappen; zwingen

geradeaus

And that is where Sheriff the carthorse always walks. Sheriff smells horrible!

So Max does not like to trot behind him.

But Max has to trot behind Sheriff: he is a fairground horse and that is his job. Max, Sheriff and the other horses visit lots of towns. All the children there think that Max is "cute". They ask their parents for money so that they can ride him.

Max does not like small children who shout loudly. But he does like the children who give him sweets. And the children who like his soft fur and his patience.

Ackergaul

riecht fürchterlich

hinter traben

Kirmespferd

besuchen

niedlich

Süßigkeiten

weiches Fell

Geduld

But Maxi is the only child who knows where Max likes to be scratched.

Maxi is sad because Max only comes to her town every six months. When he is there, she rides him, scratches him and tells him jokes. Sometimes she gives him some of her popcorn!

einzige

gekratzt werden

Witze

Maxi lives opposite the fairground.

Jahrmarkt

So she always knows when her friend Max is in town.

One day she buys a present for him.

A special hairbrush! Maxi wants to groom Max with it.

besondere Haarbürste

pflegen

Early in the morning, Maxi runs to the fairground. The roundabouts are not ready yet. Maxi doesn't look at the big wheel or the ghost train. She only wants to see Max. And when he sees her, he snorts loudly.

Jahrmarkt

Karussells

Riesenrad; Geisterbahn

schnaubt

Max sees the brush in her hand and is very happy.

Maxi asks the owner of the horses if she can groom Max. He says yes!

Max really loves it when she grooms him.

Maxi carefully brushes all the dust out of his fur. She even finds a tick on his tummy. Maxi calls ticks "little vampires". She puts a little oil onto it because she knows that ticks do not like oil. Soon the tick falls off Max.

Then Maxi takes the brush and grooms the special place on Max's back where he always has an itch. Max is so happy that he stamps with his hooves!

At last his friend Maxi is here! Maxi, the best back-scratcher in the whole world!

Bürste

Besitzer

pflegen

wirklich

bürstet vorsichtig

Staub; Fell
Zecke
Bauch

Vampire

Öl

fällt ab

besondere Stelle

Juckreiz

stampft; Hufen

Endlich

Rücken-Kratzer

ganzen

Then Maxi sees another horse behind her. It is Sheriff. He wants to be groomed as well.

"All right," Maxi says. "Wait there. I'll do you in a moment."

noch ein	
auch gepflegt werden	
In Ordnung	

Peter's pipe-cleaner horse

Fridolin the horse is not a real horse. He is made of two pipe-cleaners. A red one and a white one.

   Fridolin has long, shaggy legs and red, floppy ears. He thinks that he looks nice. He wants to go onto a big green meadow full of grass so that he can run around.

   But one day, somebody ties a plastic tube to his front leg! Fridolin is shocked.

   He wants to shout: "Hey! Stop that!" But he cannot. Because Fridolin is a pipe-cleaner horse at a shooting gallery.

   With the plastic tube on his front leg, he is put on a shelf. Beside him are some teddy bears, paper flowers and chimney sweeps.

real	echtes
is made of	ist gemacht aus
pipe-cleaners	Pfeifenputzer
shaggy	struppige
floppy ears	Schlappohren
nice	nett
meadow	Weide
ties	bindet
plastic tube	Plastikröhrchen;
front leg	Vorderbein
shocked	schockiert
shooting gallery	Schießbude
is put on	wird gestellt in;
Beside	Neben
paper flowers	Papierblumen;
chimney sweeps	Schornsteinfeger

The chimney sweep beside Fridolin is made of black pipe-cleaners.

Fridolin wants to say that horses belong on the meadow and chimney sweeps belong on the roof. But Fridolin can't say anything. He has no mouth.

*Schornsteinfeger neben;
ist gemacht aus*

Pfeifenputzer

gehören; Weide

auf das Dach

Then Fridolin sees people. They eat big white clouds on a stick. It is called candy-floss.

Wolken
Stiel; Zuckerwatte

Some people shoot little round bullets at the plastic tube on Fridolin's leg. But they don't hit it. One bullet hits Fridolin's floppy ear. It really hurts him.

schießen
runde Kugeln; Plastikröhrchen

Schlappohr
tut wirklich weh

The people fire the most bullets at the big teddy bear. The owner of the shooting gallery takes the teddy bear and gives it to a man. The man gives the teddy bear to a young woman. She kisses the bear.

schießen

Besitzer
Schießbude

"He is lucky," Fridolin thinks.

"I hope someone takes me away, too. I don't want to stay here. I want to be with people who talk to me. I want someone to kiss me, too!"

nimmt mich mit
bleiben

But the people are not very interested in Fridolin.

Fridolin gets very sad because for many days no one fires any bullets at his plastic tube. Not even by mistake.

Then little Peter arrives at the shooting gallery. Peter loves horses.

"Mummy," Peter says. "Mummy, please shoot at that nice horse for me!"

viele Tage lang

schießt; Kugeln

Plastikröhrchen
Nicht einmal aus Versehen.

Schießbude

His mother shakes her head.   *schüttelt den Kopf*

"I can't do that. I don't know how to fire a gun," she says.   *wie man mit einer Waffe schießt*

She wants to walk on but he shouts: "Please try, Mummy!"   *versuch es*

Fridolin wants her to try as well. He likes Peter.   *auch*

"Please, Mummy. I want that horse. I will never get a real one."   *echtes*

Fridolin wants to say: "Yes, take me! I'm a real pipe-cleaner horse!" But he cannot make a sound.   *Pfeifenputzer* / *Geräusch*

The owner of the shooting gallery gives the gun to Peter's mother. He winks at her.   *Besitzer* / *Schießbude* / *zwinkert zu*

Peter's mother smiles. "Well, usually men fire guns. But today I want to try as well. Here we go!"   *lächelt*

The mother picks up the gun and takes aim.   *nimmt auf* / *zielt*

Then the mother fires! And half of the plastic tube disappears! Fridolin is very happy: "I'm nearly free!"

"Well done, Mummy! Well done!" Peter laughs.

The mother is a bit shocked. She asks the gallery owner: "Do we get the little horse now?"

He shakes his head. "No. You must shoot away all of the tube."

"How much does a shot cost?"

"50 cent."

The mother shakes her head. "That's very expensive. Oh, forget it."

Peter looks inside his pocket and takes out 50 cent. He gives it to his mother.

"Please, Mummy!"

feuert ab
die Hälfte des Plastikröhrchens
verschwindet
beinahe frei
Gut gemacht
ein bisschen schockiert
Schießbudenbesitzer
schüttelt den Kopf
wegschießen
Tasche

She shakes her head. "Peter! That's all your money. What if I miss?" | schüttelt den Kopf
Was ist, wenn ich es verfehle?

"Please, Mummy!" Peter says. "You're the best mummy in the whole world." | beste
ganzen

"Oh well, all right," Peter's mother says. She picks up the gun, takes aim, fires – and hits the tube! | in Ordnung
nimmt auf
zielt; schießt
trifft

Fridolin is free!

Peter holds Fridolin in his hand and says: "For me you're a real horse!" | echtes

"But of course I'm a real horse," Fridolin says. "I'm a real pipe-cleaner horse!" | natürlich

Pfeifenputzer

Tinka and the lollipop

Julia hangs a photo on the wall. It is a picture of her first riding lesson. Julia's little sister Steffi watches her.

	Wand
	Reitstunde

Now Julia can see the photo when she goes to bed at night and when she gets up in the morning.

The horse in the photo is called Tinka. She is a small white mare. Children sometimes think she is a pony because she is so tiny. But Tinka is a real horse.

Stute

winzig

echtes

Tinka likes children. After the first riding lesson, the riding instructor usually gives the children a strawberry lollipop.
Tinka gets a reward, too.
A nice carrot because the riding instructor says that lollipops are not good for Tinka's teeth.

Reitlehrerin

Erdbeer-Lutscher

Belohnung

Möhre

Zähne

Julia likes carrots, too. That is why she secretly does a swap with Tinka. Julia eats the carrot and Tinka eats the lollipop!

The instructor notices this. She looks angry. "Don't do that again, Julia! Tinka gets toothache from lollipops!"

heimlich

tauscht

Lehrerin bemerkt

wütend

Zahnschmerzen; Lutschern

"So do I," Julia says very quietly. | *ruhig*
Tinka and Julia are good friends.

And now Tinka's photo is on the wall. | *Wand*

Julia's little sister Steffi has a photo of Fury on her wall. She is jealous of Julia because she can't ride Fury. | *eifersüchtig auf*

"I think your horse is stupid!" Steffi says. | *blöd*

"You don't know Tinka. She's the best horse in the whole world!" Julia answers. | *beste* *ganzen*

"No she isn't. Fury is much better!" | *viel* *besser*

"Fury is only on TV but Tinka is a real horse. You're just jealous because you don't know how to ride!" | *echtes*

"But I want to have lessons soon!" Steffi shouts. She is so angry that she nearly cries. | *Unterricht* *bald* *wütend; fast weint*

"Yes, when you're nine years old like me. But you're only four," Julia says.

Now Steffi cries. Julia gives her a handkerchief to wipe her nose.

"Come on," Julia says. "Arguments are silly. I want to show you Tinka tomorrow. And you can watch me ride."

cries	weint
handkerchief	Taschentuch
wipe	putzen
Arguments; silly	Streit; dumm

Steffi wipes her nose.
She is happy that she can go
with Julia. But she is still
a little bit angry because Julia
is allowed to do everything.

The next day Julia
takes her little sister to the
riding stable. The stable
smells of straw and horse.
Steffi holds Julia's hand.
The children walk past
the big horses.

Snowball, the wild stallion,
kicks the wall loudly. He is
restless. He wants to
go outside.

Now Steffi is a little bit
worried.

The horses frighten her.

Billy, the racehorse,
sticks his head out and
sniffs at Steffi's hair. Billy
loves freshly-washed hair!

putzt

ein bisschen wütend

darf

Reitstall

riecht nach Stroh

laufen vorbei an

wilde Hengst

tritt; Wand

unruhig

besorgt

machen ihr Angst

Rennpferd steckt seinen Kopf heraus

schnuppert an frisch gewaschenes

Steffi is shocked. She falls down. Billy neighs. It sounds like a laugh.

schockiert	
fällt hin; wiehert	
klingt wie ein Lachen	

The riding instructor says hello to Julia and Steffi. She notices that Steffi is frightened and gives her a red lollipop. Steffi looks at Tinka. Now the riding instructor lifts Julia onto Tinka's back.

Reitlehrerin

bemerkt

fürchtet sich

Lutscher

hebt; Rücken

Steffi is surprised. Tinka is so big!

überrascht

Perhaps she bites!

Vielleicht; beißt

The riding instructor says to Steffi: "Don't worry. You can stroke Tinka."

Keine Angst.

streicheln

But Steffi is still frightened. Then Tinka looks down and puts her mouth next to Steffi's face. Steffi can feel her warm breath. She does not dare to move.

neben

warmen Atem

wagt

"She wants to bite me! Help!" Steffi says. She is scared.

hat Angst

But Tinka wants the red lollipop in Steffi's hand. The mare takes it in her mouth and eats it.

Steffi laughs. She touches Tinka on the mouth. The skin is very soft and warm.

Tinka touches Steffi's face with her big, soft nose.

"Hey, Steffi," the riding instructor says. "Where is your lolly?"

"It's in Tinka's tummy!"

"That doesn't matter," the riding instructor laughs. "You can have Tinka's carrot instead."

Tinka neighs and licks Steffi's face!

lollipop	Lutscher
mare	Stute
touches	berührt
skin	Haut
soft	weich
riding instructor	Reitlehrerin
tummy	Bauch
That doesn't matter	Das macht nichts
instead	stattdessen
neighs	wiehert
licks	leckt

Prinz and the horse with horns

It is a hot summer day.   heißer
   Prinz walks across his meadow. He snorts, and   Weide; schnaubt
the wind blows the hair   weht
of his mane.   Mähne
   The cows in the field   Kühe
beside him look at him.   neben
They feel jealous. They   eifersüchtig
want lots of room, too.   viel Platz

The five cows stand in their meadow. The meadow is too small. Prinz has a big meadow all to himself!

The cows have to drink rainwater out of a trough. Prinz has a little brook in his meadow with deliciously fresh mountain water.

When the weather is hot, the cows' drinking water gets much too warm. Today it does not taste nice.

Weide

ganz für sich (allein)

Trog

Bach

köstlich frischem

Wetter; heiß

schmeckt

Prinz stands in the brook and drinks the cool water. Delicious!   *Bach*   *kalte; Köstlich!*

Prinz is lucky. But he is jealous of the cows. There are five of them but he is always alone. Except on Sunday when his owner comes to saddle him and ride him.   *eifersüchtig auf*   *allein; Außer*   *Besitzer*   *satteln*

Prinz is also a bit frightened of the cows. They have horns and look like devils.   *fürchtet sich auch ein bisschen*   *Hörner*   *Teufel*

Prinz is also jealous of the apple tree in the cows' meadow. He likes apples.   *Weide*

Today is a special day. Berta, the fat cow, talks to a horse for the first time in her life.   *besonderer*   *dicke*   *Leben*

She stands by the fence, looks at Prinz, and says: "Hello, Prinz. My name is Berta. If you give me some of your fresh water, I can give you an apple."   *Zaun*   *frischen*

All that Prinz can understand is "Mooo! Moooo!"

He is worried and says to Berta: "I don't hurt you so you mustn't hurt me!"

For Berta this sounds like: "Neiiigh! Neiiigh!"

"You're a bit stupid," Berta says. "I can't understand a word you say."

Muh!

besorgt

wehtun

klingt

Wieher!

blöd

All that Prinz can hear is: "Mooo!"   *Muh!*

Prinz is frightened of Berta's horns. "She wants to hurt me," he thinks, and runs away to the corner of his meadow.   *fürchtet sich / Hörnern; wehtun / Ecke; Weide*

Berta thinks this is an invitation. Part of the fence is a bit broken. She tells the other cows to knock it down so they can drink the delicious water.   *Einladung / Zaun; ein bisschen kaputt / ihn niedertrampeln / köstliche*

"Let's bring him some apples," Berta's sister Anneliese says. They pick up some apples with their teeth but are so thirsty for water that they eat them.   *Zähnen; durstig*

Then Berta and her friends knock down the fence.

Prinz is terrified. He starts to neigh: "Help! The horses with the devil horns! They want to hurt me!" But the cows do not hurt him.   *hat fürchterliche Angst / wiehern / Teufelshörnern*

Anneliese comes towards Prinz. She has an apple in her mouth. Prinz is very scared.

Then Anneliese rolls the apple towards his hoof and he suddenly understands: the cows are not devils. They are not dangerous at all!

Day after day Prinz's master mends the fence. But the cows always knock it down again, and Prinz is not alone anymore.

auf ... zu	
hat große Angst	
Huf	
plötzlich	
Teufel	
überhaupt nicht gefährlich	
Tag für Tag; Besitzer	
repariert; Zaun	
trampeln ihn nieder	
nicht mehr allein	

Jan looks after the horses

Jan is a boy with red hair. He likes to stand by the fence and look at the horses in the meadow. He knows all their names.

There are twelve horses altogether. And there are also two foals called Luntrus and Ajax. They are eight weeks old.

Zaun

Weide

Fohlen

fence

The foals have long, wobbly legs. They look funny.

Jan's favourite horse is Fury. Fury is as black as night, and he has a clever look in his eyes.

Fury is the fastest horse in the meadow. He likes to race along beside the cars that drive past. Jan likes to watch him. He tells Fury to run even faster!

Fohlen; wackelige	
lustig	
Lieblingspferd	
klugen Blick	
schnellste	
Weide	
nebenherrennen	
vorbeifahren	
noch schneller	

foal

"*Faster*, Fury! You can *easily beat* that Mercedes! Faster!" | *Schneller leicht schlagen*

The *meadow* is big and long. Fury *gallops a long way*, but the cars usually win. | *Weide gallopiert eine lange Strecke*

The car drivers *travel by* very quickly. They do not see the horses. But the children in the *back seats* like to look at the horses. And *especially* at Fury. | *vorbeifahren* / *Rücksitzen* / *besonders*

Jan's parents are not very happy because he *spends* all day at the meadow. They think it is *too close to* the road and the cars. | *verbringt* / *zu nahe an*

"One day someone will *run you over*!" Jan's father often says. "The road is *much too close* to the meadow." | *dich überfahren* / *viel zu nahe*

But Jan knows how *to take care of himself*. | *auf sich selbst aufpassen*

Today something is wrong.
The horses are very nervous.
They run along the fence. They
are worried about something.
Jan is curious.
What is the matter?
Fury stands on his hind legs
and neighs.

aufgeregt
rennen entlang;
Zaun

besorgt über

neugierig

Was ist los?

Hinterbeinen

wiehert

His neigh sounds different as well. It sounds a bit like a warning. Like Jan's father's voice when he says: "One day someone will run you over!"

Then Jan sees why the horses are so nervous: part of the fence is broken! The wood is smashed. A car must have crashed into it.

Jan suddenly realizes the danger. The horses can escape now and run onto the road!

Jan is shocked. Where are the foals? He sees Ajax but Luntrus is gone!

"What can I do?" Jan wonders. What if Luntrus is on the other side of the hole in the fence? Suddenly Jan is very frightened. Perhaps Luntrus is in the middle of the road!

Wiehern klingt auch anders	
Warnung; Stimme	
aufgeregt	
Zaun; kaputt	
Holz; zerbrochen	
Ein Auto muss hineingerast sein.	
begreift plötzlich Gefahr; entkommen	
schockiert	
Fohlen	
weg	
fragt sich auf der anderen Seite	
Loch	
fürchtet sich	
Vielleicht	
mitten auf	

Then Jan hears a car horn. | Hupe
He runs off as fast as he can to the stable! | rennt los / Stall
Fury runs along beside him. | rennt nebenher
Jan shouts: "Mr Reuter! Mr Reuter! The fence is broken! | Zaun; kaputt
Luntrus is in the middle of the road! He is all alone!" | mitten auf / ganz allein

Mr Reuter hears Jan's shouts. He immediately starts to run towards the road as fast as he can. | sofort

"Stay with the horses so that no more of them escape!" he shouts to Jan. "I will get Luntrus!"

Jan blocks the horses' way.

Bleib bei

keines mehr
Ich werde schnappen

versperrt; Weg

But the horses stay in the meadow. | bleiben
| Weide

Half an hour later, Mr Reuter comes back with Luntrus. Mr Reuter's face is red. | Eine halbe Stunde später

He says to Jan: "I must mend that fence." | reparieren
| Zaun

He chases Luntrus back into the meadow. | jagt

Then he takes Jan's hand and thanks him: "You are a very good guard, Jan. Thank you very much. | Aufpasser

When Luntrus is bigger, you can ride him. If you like." | größer

The tracker

Every Sunday, Arno goes for a walk with his parents. He thinks it is boring. His father and mother want to build a house, and they only talk about the house.   *geht spazieren* / *langweilig* / *bauen*

Arno's father says that he wants red tiles on the roof. His mother says that she wants black slate instead.   *Ziegel* / *Schiefer* / *stattdessen*

Arno is unhappy. He is not interesting for them.   *unglücklich*

Then suddenly he finds a horseshoe.   *plötzlich* / *Hufeisen*

People say that horseshoes bring good luck.   *bringen Glück*

Arno wants to show it to his parents. But they only talk about the house they want to build.

"Oh well, never mind," Arno thinks, and he puts the horseshoe in his pocket.   *dann eben nicht* / *Tasche*

Arno looks at the ground. He can see the hoof-prints of horses. He follows them like an Indian tracker. The prints come from lots of horses. At least three. One of them lost its horseshoe.

Arno can see this clearly. One track is different from the other ones.

Boden	
Hufabdrücke	
folgt	
indianischer Fährtensucher	
Mindestens	
verlor; Hufeisen	
deutlich	
Spur; anders als	

He sees three hoof-prints
with horseshoe shapes,
and one print from the horse's
foot without the shoe.

Arno feels like a real tracker
from a Western film. Suddenly,
the Sunday walk is not boring.

The tracks of one horse
turn left into the forest. The
others stay on the path.

Hufabdrücke	
Hufeisen-Form	
echter Fährtenleser	
Plötzlich	
langweilig	
Spuren	
biegen links ab	
Pfad	

A few metres further, the tracks come together again. But now Arno sees footprints beside the hoof-prints.
   The footprints are from the rider of the horse.
   Arno follows the footprints further. Then suddenly they stop. That means the rider is back in the saddle again.

Einige Meter weiter	
Fußabdrücke neben; Hufabdrücken	
folgt	
weiter; plötzlich	
bedeutet	
Sattel	

hoof-prints

But then Arno sees
something else.   *noch etwas*

He sees dark stains inside   *dunkle Flecken*
the hoof-prints. He sees
what it is: blood.   *Blut*

The horse does
not have its shoe anymore,   *nicht mehr*
but it is also injured!   *verletzt*

When Arno gets to the
top of the hill, he sees   *Hügelspitze*
three riders in the valley.   *Tal*

His father and mother want to
sit down on a bench and   *Bank*
have a rest. Arno runs down   *Pause*
to the riders in the valley.

"Your horse has lost a shoe!"   *hat verloren*
he shouts. "And it is injured!   *verletzt*
Come and look!"

The rider takes a close look   *sieht genau an*
at his horse's foot.

"You're right! Joker is
injured!" the rider says.

So the horse's name is Joker.

Arno strokes the horse. — streichelt
The rider allows Arno to — erlaubt
keep the horseshoe. — behalten; Hufeisen

Arno goes back to his parents. They argue about — streiten um
the colour of the tiles in — Fliesen
the bathroom.

Arno does not listen to them.

He decides to hang the — beschließt
horseshoe on the wall of — Wand
his new bedroom.

Then he goes into the forest to look for more tracks. — Spuren

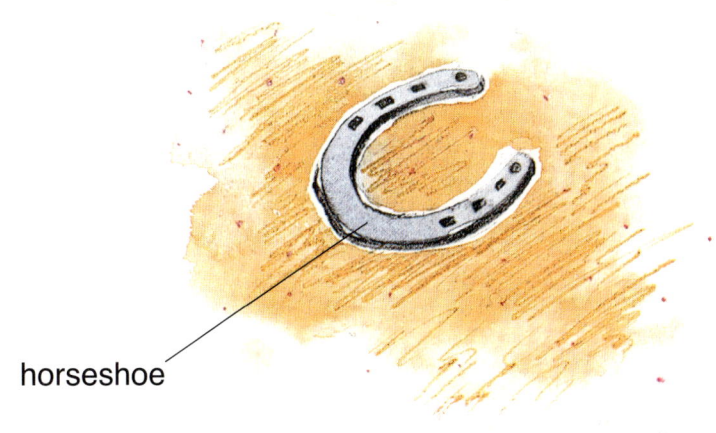

horseshoe

Dein Wörterbuch A–H

A
again	noch einmal, wieder
a little bit	ein kleines bisschen
all alone	ganz allein
all right	in Ordnung
alone	allein
angry	wütend
another	noch eine, -r, -s, ein anderer
(not) anymore	nicht mehr
to argue about	streiten um
as well	auch
at last	endlich, schließlich
at least	wenigstens, mindestens

B
to be allowed to	dürfen
to be called	heißen
to be frightened	sich fürchten
behind	hinter
to belong	gehören
beside	neben
broken	kaputt

C
clearly	deutlich
corner	Ecke

	curious	neugierig
D	to dare	wagen, herausfordern
	to decide	sich entscheiden, beschließen
	different from	anders als
	to disappear	verschwinden
	Don't worry!	Keine Angst!, keine Sorge
E	each	jede, -r, -s
	easily	leicht
	to escape	entkommen, entfliehen
	especially	besonders
	even faster	noch schneller
	except	außer
F	to follow	(ver-)folgen, nachkommen
G	to go for a walk	spazieren gehen
	gone	weg, vergangen, vorbei
H	half	halb, die Hälfte, zur Hälfte
	handkerchief	Taschentuch
	to hope	hoffen

Dein Wörterbuch H–S

H	horrible	schrecklich, furchtbar
	hot	heiß
I	to ignore	nicht beachten
	immediately	sofort
	instead of	stattdessen, anstelle von
	in the middle of	mitten auf, in
	it doesn't matter	das macht nichts
K	to keep	(be-)halten, weitermachen, bleiben
L	later	später
	life	Leben
	like me	wie ich
	like this	so, auf diese Weise
M	to mean	bedeuten, meinen,
	much better	viel besser
N	to need	brauchen, müssen
	nervous	aufgeregt
	never mind	dann eben nicht, macht nichts

	no more	kein, -e, -r, -s mehr
	to nod	nicken
	not even	nicht einmal
O	of course	selbstverständlich
	only	einzige, -r, -s, nur
P	perhaps	vielleicht
R	real	echt, wirklich
	to realize	erkennen, begreifen, bemerken, verwirklichen
	right in front of	direkt vor
	to run along	entlangrennen
	to run into	rennen in, rennen gegen
	to run off	wegrennen, losrennen
	to run down	hinunterrennen
S	secretly	heimlich
	shocked	schockiert
	silly	dumm
	to smell	riechen
	to smile	lächeln

Dein Wörterbuch S–W

S	soon	bald
	sound	Geräusch
	special	besondere, -r, -s
	to spend	verbringen
	to stay	bleiben
	stupid	dumm
	suddenly	plötzlich
	surprised	überrascht
T	to take care of	aufpassen auf
	to taste	schmecken
	terrible	schrecklich, fürchterlich
	the most	die meisten
	tiny	winzig
	to try	versuchen
V	very well	sehr gut
	to visit	besuchen
W	to walk past	vorbeilaufen
	wall	Wand